Mar. 10 '93

I Remember When

Other books by
Lynne Alpern and Esther Blumenfeld:

Oh, Lord, It's Monday Again

Oh, Lord, I Sound Just Like Mama

In-Laws, Outlaws, & Other Theories of Relativity

Mama's Cooking:
Celebrities Remember Mama's Best Recipes

The Smile Connection:
How to Use Humor in Dealing with People

Other books illustrated by Cal Warlick:

Oh, Lord, It's Monday Again and
In-Laws, Outlaws, & Other Theories of Relativity
by Lynne Alpern and Esther Blumenfeld

My Grandmother Died Again by Warren Blumenfeld

Sex, Wealth & Power by Jerry Farber

Out of My Head by LeRoy Powell

I Remember
WHEN...

Lynne Alpern and Esther Blumenfeld
Illustrated by Cal Warlick

PEACHTREE PUBLISHERS, LTD.

Atlanta

Published by
Peachtree Publishers, Ltd.
494 Armour Circle, NE
Atlanta, Georgia 30324

The illustrations in this book were rendered on
Strathmore cold press in pencil and charcoal.

Cover Design and composition by Laurie Warlick

Manufactured in the United States of America

10 9 8 7 6 5 4 3 2 1

Library of Congress Cataloging in Publication Data
Alpern, Lynne.
    I remember when— / Lynne Alpern and Esther Blumenfeld:
illustrated by Cal Warlick.
        p. cm.
    ISBN 1-56145-081-2
    1. American wit and humor.   I. Blumenfeld, Esther. II. Title.
    PN6162.A42   1993
818' .540208—dc20
                                                                    92-38297
                                                                        CIP

Dedication

For Warren and Josh and a lifetime of other
astonishing friendships. Oh, do I remember when...

Esther

To all my friends in Houston from my first childhood,
And to Bob, Eve, and Ken, who are creating the
memories for my second one...

Lynne

Introduction

Fairy tales begin with "Once upon a time...." But real-life stories spring from "I remember when...." And what follows those three words can teach, frighten, titillate, or spark the knowing laughter of recognition in folks who think they've heard it all before.

Childhood memories have added to the chronicle of history, provided drama in the courtroom, and inspired both the novelist and the poet. One person's retrospection usually triggers similar thoughts in your mind of events long past: imaginary friends...school plays...first dates. And each memory is as unique as the person who lived it, relates it, and, perhaps, embellishes it.

"I remember when I spent the night at a friend's house for the first time, and I didn't even make it past dinner."

"I remember when the neighborhood kids always came to my house to play 'cause dad was the most fun kid on the block."

"I remember when no day was complete without managing to tease a whine attack out of my little sister."

"I remember when the movie got too mushy and we'd stick fingers down our throats and make gagging sounds."

"I remember when grandmothers used to have white hair and big laps."

Next time there's a lull in the conversation, ask, "What's the dumbest thing you ever did growing up?" and your friends will immediately be awash in alternating waves of nostalgia and laughter. Because all of life is two-sided—the light-hearted and the melancholy.

Since this is our book, however, we flipped the coin of remembrance past, and ours landed on the sweet and funny side. We hope the side we bring you will warm your hearts and make you laugh as it reminds you joyfully of events long forgotten.

So stick your toes in a stream of childhood recollections and...remember when....

I remember when...

...I cut my hair and had a bald spot just like Daddy's.

...I used to hide in fancy Aunt Noonie's closet so I could play puppet with the heads of her fox stole.

...I was always hollering, "Hey you guys, wait for me!"

...I was shocked when my teacher told us she was moving to a new house, because I always thought she lived at school.

...I first realized that Grandmother was once a little girl.

...my aunt took all the monsters out of my bedroom closet, packed them in her suitcase, and took them home with her.

...it rained all week, and my desperate Mom threw a blanket over the grand piano and we all ate hot dogs in our tent.

...we played hide 'n seek with the baby-sitter and managed not to find her until all the ice cream was gone.

...Mom would say, "Wait 'til your father gets home," and when he got home she'd be so happy to see him, she'd forget that she had said it.

...I stood on Daddy's feet, and we danced at my cousin's wedding until his knees locked.

...my gerbil died while the minister was visiting, and we all bowed our heads as he solemnly lowered "Jerkie" into the garbage can.

...my sister explained the birds and the bees to me, and I didn't believe her.

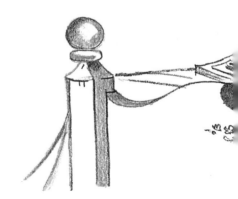

…my best friend and I concocted a salami, sardine, cheese, jelly, olive, and peanut butter sandwich and convinced my little brother it would give him muscles.

...to prove to your friends you were really smart, you did something really stupid.

…my cousin dared me to lick the front doorknob and my tongue got frozen stuck.

...my brother and I licked all the fillings out of the Oreo cookies and then glued them back together with cream cheese.

...lying on the grass and staring up at the clouds was enough to fill up a whole afternoon of wondering.

…we knew we never had to come in for dinner until Mom used her "I-mean-it" voice.

...I made a lopsided footstool in shop class, and my mother wedged it's pegleg into one of Dad's old Meerschaum pipes and proudly used it for 45 years.

...Dad yelled at my best friend and me to stop fighting and shake hands, and we would squeeze and squeeze until he yelled at us again to let go.

...I was baby sitting with little Pearl Ann, and I knew I was grown up because I was the one who had to squash the spider.

...I paid my brother $2 to take the blame for a broken lamp because I had already passed my limit for breaking the house that week.

...Mama used to sigh, "Haven't you practiced the piano enough?"

...my grandma would stop traffic by slapping cars with her umbrella so we could cross the street.

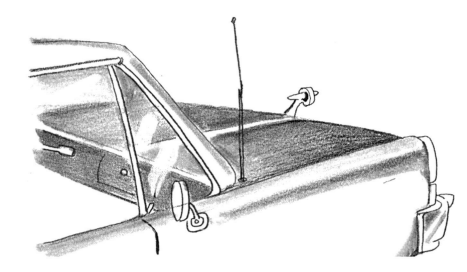

PUSH
BUTTON
FOR
LIGHT

...all the anatomy my best friend and I knew, we learned from the girdle ads in the Sears catalog.

...all my friends had a crush on my big brother and I thought they were nuts.

...my sister thought we were fooling mom by smoking in the bathroom with the window wide open.

...I wrote down everything I needed to say to ask a girl out, called, and read the whole shebang aloud before realizing I had just invited her mother to the Prom.

...my little brother would answer the phone and tell my boyfriends exactly where I was and what I was doing at that moment.

...I knew I finally had a real date. My mom didn't drive us there, and her mom didn't drive us home.

...I had the housekey clutched in my sweaty palm before my date even pulled away from the malt shop.

...I couldn't figure out where the noses went when you kissed.

...we decorated the gym for our Junior Prom. It looked like a fairyland but still smelled like a gym.

I remember when...

...I NEVER FORGOT
WHAT I HAD TO REMEMBER.

About the Authors:

In addition to I REMEMBER WHEN, Lynne Alpern and Esther Blumenfeld are the authors of five books: OH, LORD, IT'S MONDAY AGAIN; IN-LAWS, OUTLAWS & *Other Theories of Relativity;* MAMA'S COOKING: *Celebrities Remember Mama's Best Recipes;* OH, LORD, I SOUND JUST LIKE MAMA; and THE SMILE CONNECTION: *How to Use Humor in Dealing with People*, for which they were named Authors of the Year in Humor for 1986 by the Council of Authors and Journalists.

Alpern and Blumenfeld have also published over 200 articles and are former contributing editors to *Busizness Atlanta* magazine. They conduct workshops on humor for business and conventions and have been featured on numerous radio and television programs in the U.S. and Canada. For five years, their humor awareness course has been offered at Emory University. They also teach courses in humor writing and have been guest faculty at summer writers' conferences.

About the Illustrator:

Cal Warlick is a freelance illustrator in Atlanta and former Creative Director and editorial cartoonist for the *Gwinnett Daily News*. He has received numerous awards for his work, including eight Emmy awards from the Georgia Chapter of the National Academy of Television Arts and Sciences. His illustrations and editorial cartoons have also been honored by the Broadcast Designers Association, Suburban Newspapers of America, and the Georgia Press Association. He has previously illustrated OH, LORD, IT'S MONDAY AGAIN; SEX, WEALTH, & POWER: *How to Live Without Them;* MY GRANDMOTHER DIED AGAIN & *Other Almost Believable Excuses*; IN-LAWS, OUTLAWS & *Other Theories of Relativity;* and OUT OF MY HEAD: *Coon Dogs That Lie to You, Killer Pancakes & Other Lunacies.*